MARCH WITH MARSHA

written by Katie Hall
illustrated by Veronica V. Jones

Text Copyright 2020 © by Katie Hall
Illustration Copyright 2020 © by Veronica V. Jones
ISBN: 978-0-578-55647-5
ebook ISBN: 978-1-087-85600-1
All rights reserved.

History and Vocabulary

"Queer" is used in this book as an umbrella term for the LGBTQ+ community. The community at the Stonewall Inn was a diverse group of people who had been largely rejected by society: trans people, effeminate men, butch lesbians, drag queens, sex workers, and homeless queer youth. Marsha and Sylvia both identified themselves as transvestites. In contemporary LGBTQ+ vocabulary, they are usually described as trans women.

After the Stonewall Riots, Marsha and Sylvia formed the Street Transvestites Action Revolutionaries (STAR). This organization provided political advocacy and housing for homeless queer youth and sex workers - a community much like the one that had previously found a home at Stonewall.

The Stonewall Riots were a tipping point for LGBTQ+ people all across the country to stand up and resist oppression based on their gender identity or sexual orientation.

June 28, 1969

Marsha P. Johnson is 25 years old, and today she celebrates her birthday.

Happy birthday, Marsha!

Police enforce the laws. They want to punish Marsha for being Marsha. They want to punish Marsha's friends for being themselves too.

The police come to the Stonewall Inn. They arrest people for being there.

Marsha and her friends know this is wrong. They know they should be free to be themselves.

"Why doesn't somebody do something?" one woman asks.

Marsha's friend Sylvia Rivera is tired of being treated like dirt.

Sylvia decides to do something. She throws a bottle at the police.

They hear about the Stonewall Inn. They hear how brave Marsha and her friends are.

They can be brave too! Brave like Marsha.

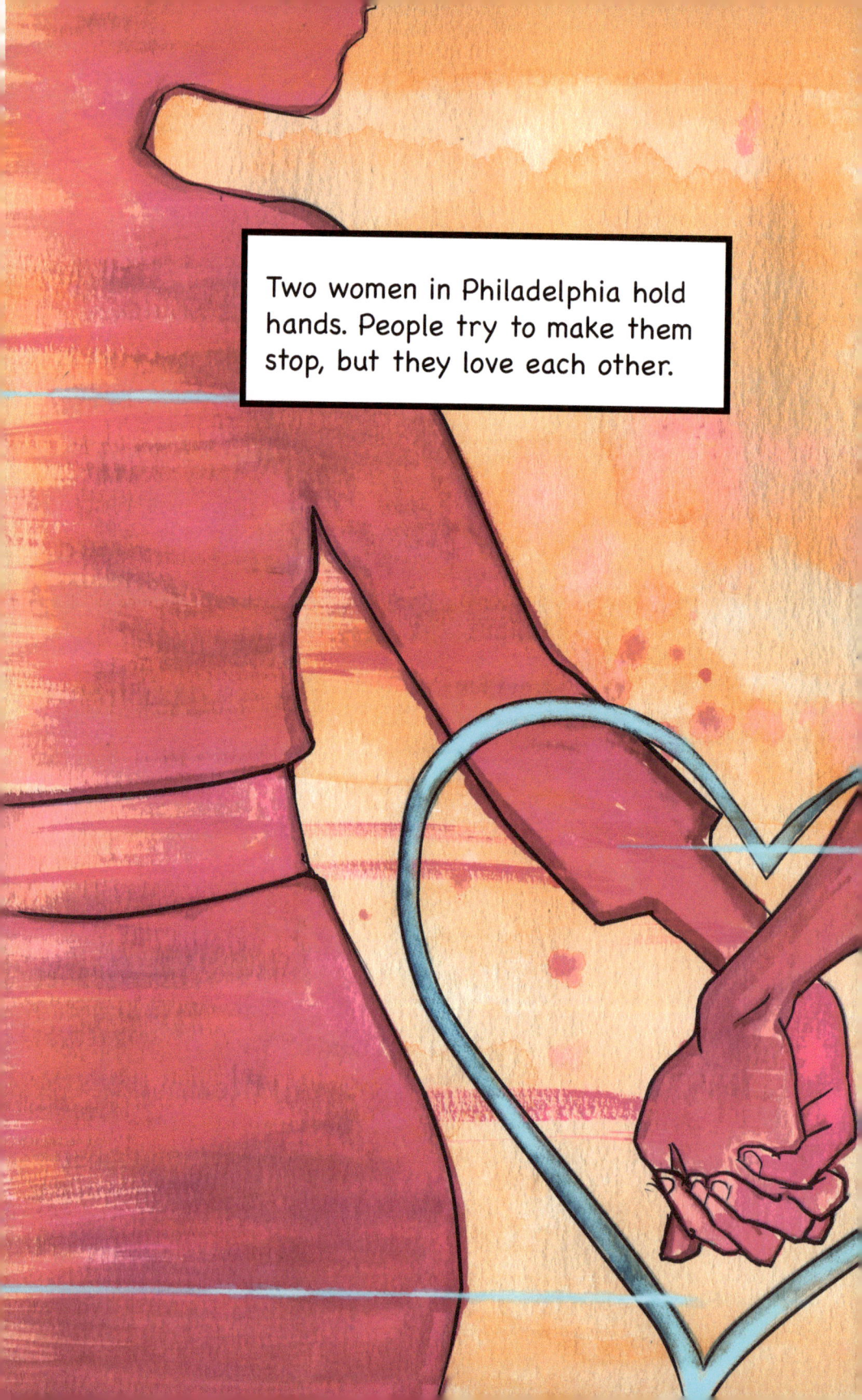

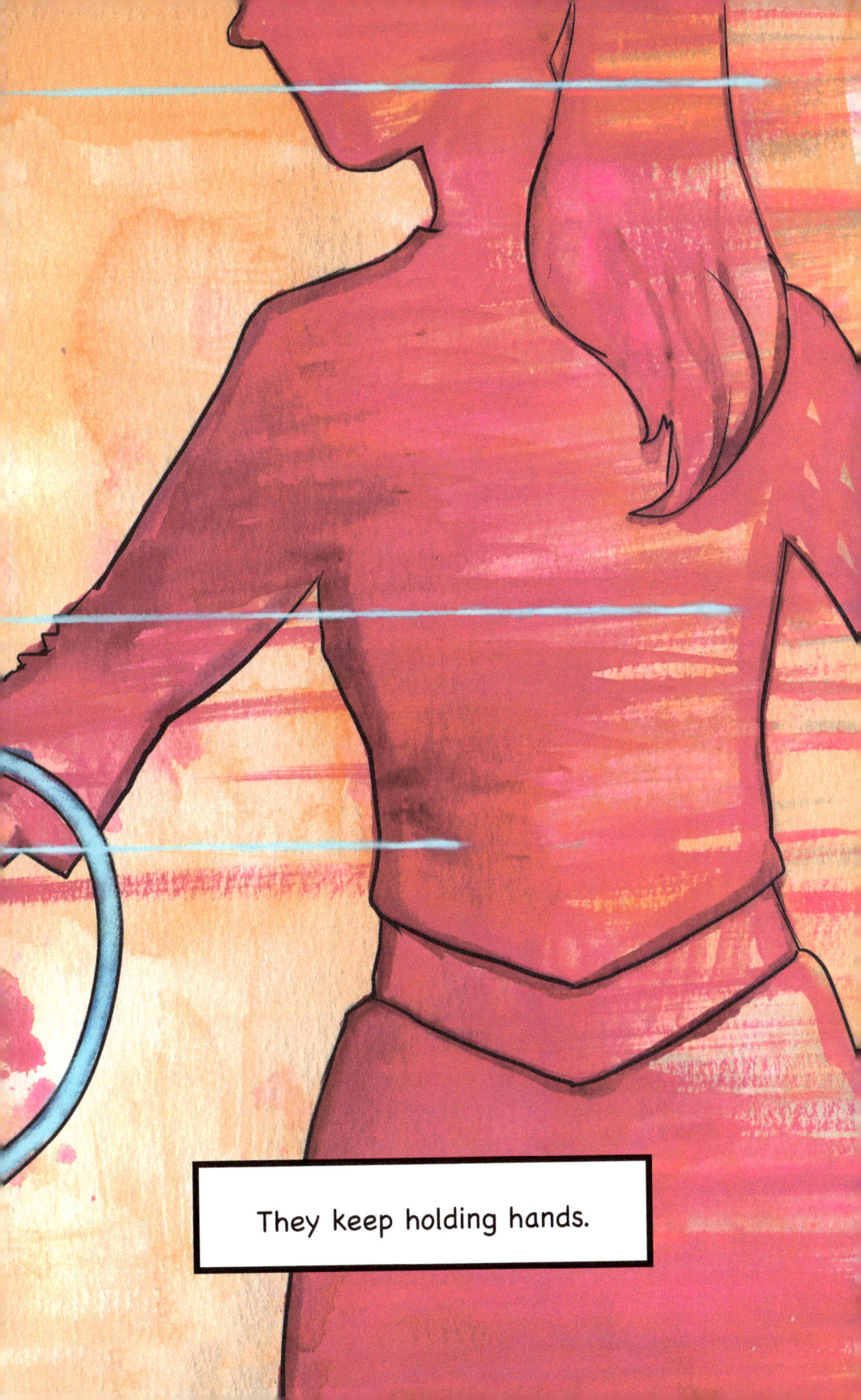

Marsha and Sylvia start a new organization to help young people like themselves. They march and organize and stand up for queer people's rights.

Katie Hall is an award-winning author and former children's book editor. Katie is excited to use their passion and experience to introduce children to often-overlooked heroes who have led the way in the fight for equal rights. Some of their previous works include *Polar Bears and Penguins: A Compare and Contrast Book* (NSTA/CBC Outstanding Science Trade Book and ILA Children's and Young Adult Award for Primary Nonfiction), *Amphibians and Reptiles*, and *Mammals*. Katie lives in South Carolina with their family of humans, dogs, and cats. Visit their website at www.kghall.net.

As a child, **Veronica V. Jones** enjoyed reading comic books with her dad; this started a lifelong love of reading stories and creating art. After graduating from college, she pursued a career as an illustrator. Veronica first worked in the tabletop games industry and then started drawing for children in 2010. Since then, she has worked on covers and interiors for middle grade novels as well as picture books for younger children. When not drawing and painting, Veronica keeps very busy with her two kids, taking them to lessons and practices. She is a proud leader of her daughter's Girl Scout troop.

Thanks to our Kickstarter donors, without whom this book would not have been possible: Amanita K. Hall ~ Jennifer & Sean Rahner ~ Scott Ferrell, Jr. ~ Rathmell Family ~ Michelle Haynes ~ Todd and Betsy Hintzmann ~ Gabriel de los Angeles, son of Chief Andy de los Angeles ~ Alex Riviere ~ Ash Meyer ~ Daneen Akers ~ Elizabeth Sweeny ~ Ellen ~ J Carroll ~ J. Kusluch ~ Jaime Elias Vazquez ~ Jeff Jones ~ Kit ~ Maxine ~ Natalie Pudim ~ Nate D. ~ The Bushyager Family ~ The Nester Family ~ Rebecca Hofmann ~ AleksGhost ~ Matt Johnson ~ Paula Z ~ Chelsea Allen ~ and others who chose to remain nameless

www.ingramcontent.com/pod-product-compliance
Lightning Source LLC
Chambersburg PA
CBHW041352290426
44108CB00001B/22